BLACK APERTURE

BLACK APERTURE

POEMS

. . . .

MATT RASMUSSEN

Louisiana State University Press
Baton Rouge

Published by Louisiana State University Press
Copyright © 2013 by Matt Rasmussen
All rights reserved
Manufactured in the United States of America
LSU Press Paperback Original
First printing

Designer: Barbara Neely Bourgoyne
Typefaces: News Gothic, display; Ingeborg, text
Printer and binder: IBT Global

Matt Rasmussen is a fiscal year 2011 recipient of an Artist Initiative grant from the Minnesota States Arts Board.

Library of Congress Cataloging-in-Publication Data
Rasmussen, Matt.
  [Poems. Selections]
  Black aperture : poems / Matt Rasmussen.
    pages cm
  "LSU Press Paperback Original."
  ISBN 978-0-8071-5086-3 (pbk. : alk. paper) — ISBN 978-0-8071-5087-0
(pdf) — ISBN 978-0-8071-5088-7 (epub) — ISBN 978-0-8071-5089-4 (mobi)
  I. Title.
  PS3618.A775B53 2013
  811'.6—dc23

                                                              2012038045

The paper in this book meets the guidelines for permanence
and durability of the Committee on Production Guidelines for
Book Longevity of the Council on Library Resources.
∞

for Mom and Dad

CONTENTS

I

TRAJECTORY

After spiraling twice
it exits the barrel,

the spent day exposing
a flame that propels it.

The bullet, spinning
to maintain a shallow arc,

carves a hot thread
through the wind

until it breaks one hair
and the deer's neck

splashes open.
Before the heart beats

the bullet unfolds
a plowing lead point

then again is in flight
wobbling from its passage

through the deer.
Its peeled-back body

comes to rest in the soft trunk
of a poplar to stick out

like a button. When I press it
all the leaves fall.

AFTER SUICIDE

A hole is nothing
but what remains around it.

My brother stood
in the refrigerator light

drinking milk that poured
out of his head

through thick black curls
down his back into a puddle

growing larger around him.
My body stood between the

living room and kitchen
one foot on worn carpet

one on cold linoleum.
He couldn't hear his name

clouding from my mouth
settling in the fluorescent air.

I wanted to put my finger
into the hole

feel the smooth channel
he escaped through

stop the milk
so he could swallow it

but my body held
as if driven into place.

The milk on the floor
reflected the light

then became it.
Floated upward and outward

filling every shadow
blowing the dark open.

THE ORANGE LEAVES

rocked back and forth
through the air
as if someone was

scraping the rust
off the sunset.
The chair we doused

in gasoline burned,
howling from the corner
of the field.

Its flame bent
sideways in the wind,
touched the tall

dry grass, and
the entire meadow
burned until it was black

as a parking lot.
Walking across
its smoldering coat

we found a
white deer antler
that refused to burn

and some chromed
beer cans that blew
away as we neared.

The huddling evergreens
turned their backs
and kept to themselves.

The field's remaining embers,
drawn upward, were pieces
of the evening moon

leaving for home.

747

The man who
drew the first

map was able
to see through

the eye
of a bird.

Fields speckled
with snow

are covered
in clouds

like dark faces
veiled twice.

I have told
you too much,

forgive us both.
O sun,

O stainless fuselage,
weave us

between the veils
before we darken

and dip into
the twinkling net.

Each small town
a blemish

on the night's skin,
each city

a tumor of light.

THE WAVE

He saw it everywhere.
The inevitable folding of a wave,

the patient flood of lava
traveling toward him.

He saw birds die in flight,
felt a leaf release itself in his stomach.

We become rock, he thought.
The sun, somewhere, is always rising

and setting. The earth bubbles,
driving a volcanic neck

smoking from the ocean.
No island is an island,

he said. There is no new land,
just the same body broken open.

AND GOD SAID,

Turn the sky into water.
All the animals gathered

and decided if the sky
were water they would

be drowned. So they cried
until the oceans formed.

*You have not turned
the sky into water,*

said God. *But we
have made a sky of water*

*in which fish swim
as birds fly. It is only*

a matter of perspective,
said one of the animals.

God, who was trapped
in the sky, needed a way out.

When he looked down
on the ocean he could only see

his wide blue reflection.
This irritated him.

The mountains,
which once caressed,

now ground against him.
And God said,

Tear down the mountains
and build me some fields.

The animals gathered
and having cried enough

would never again.
God knew he had

asked too much.
He threw himself

into the sun and burnt
into white ash. It fell

from the sky and covered
the mountains. The animal

who named everything
called it snow.

I AM NOT A POEM

said the poem before it leapt
from the mind, having paced

the top floor too long.
The sun always set,

but to the poem it seemed a body
floating on its own blood.

The poem saw a snowflake
and wanted to melt it. It felt

a river moving under the ice
like a rope through a frozen glove.

Through the mirror, it saw a house
of air falling inward. The poem heard

the poet calling and it jumped.

TOM BLACK

pushed me into my locker
right after I found out

my brother had killed himself.
He didn't know yet.

A few years later,
a winter dusk in the field

behind our high school:
he, too, pushed a cold trigger.

The next night I walked
through snow to where

the northern lights
fell over the dead field.

The sky crackled in blue ash
above the police ribbon

strung around some stakes.
His sprawled imprint

had melted a little.
It looked like his life

had fallen asleep.
On the white plate

my flashlight made
on the snowfield, the blood

flickered. I turned
my light off and cried.

FIELD WITH WHALES

The hunters lie down
in a cold field, their breath

pluming like a pod of whales.
A boat unzips the river

between the houses pinned
to their long shadows.

Jabbed through the sky
the moon accuses everyone.

The paper mill glugs
tan clouds into the twilight.

Dawn falls to day, but something
has been nailed to the air

informing us of our wrongs.
They turn into the breeze,

toward the cool future. You can cut
a cloud open but no love will spill.

A boy sprints through birches,
enters a clearing, becomes a deer.

AFTER SUICIDE

In the hallway of life
you were a rose with no stem

and I, the janitor sweeping
away the fallen petals.

You said the world revolves
while we ourselves remain

in the darkness of the never-
ending, never-beginning never.

I say that the man who
was humiliated in the second act

and shot himself in the fifth,
stands up, smiles, bows.

The lamp asks,
is it the shadow writing this,

the pen, or their converging?
The paper asks nothing.

IN WHOEVER'S HOTEL ROOM THIS IS

If it were up to me,
the Bible would begin:

"A man steps into a field . . ."
I'd forgotten what was in

the background when you took
the photo of me I wouldn't

see until later. When I did,
it was just a wall, and my smile

was a mouthful of rocks.
A little after it was clicked off,

the TV screen's light
condensed down a drain.

Even when the television
had become an aquarium

full of black water
that last bright dot

burned in my eye.
On the back of my photo

you wrote, *This isn't you,*
and you were right,

it no longer was.

VACATION CAGE

When you click and drag
yourself across the world

there is always the dull
remainder of the original

left behind. Not as bright
as what's moving on.

A thin curtain of pixels
clings like a spider's molt.

In a new city, a webcam
no one watches is watching

you and you feel the terrible
vacuum between lens

and audience. You laugh,
but no one laughs back.

A life is lead by learning,
before each breath,

how to breathe. You sit down.
You're either a sheet of glass

turning back into sand
or a suit woven of smoke.

The concept of time starts over.

MONET AS A VERB

The raindrop
that splatters

on a blade
of grass is

no more
worshipped

than the one
that dies

crashing against
the zinc lid

of a garbage can
or the one

after another
that Monet the

city behind
the window.

WE'RE NOT THE STARS, WE'RE WHAT'S BETWEEN THEM

A clay pigeon landed on my sill
and told me this story:

When the earth rolled on top of the sun
and crushed it into gleaming sand,

all of the world's sadness
pooled in one man's lower eyelid.

He cried the tear that sparked the flood.
A sunset is powerful, he explained.

The clay pigeon continued:
When the sadness spilled over

everyone drowned except us.
It poured into us like ink

through our eyes.
The black yolk of the pupil

is a small pool peeking out.
Then, as had always happened,

the clay pigeon flew away
and shattered in mid-air,

and I wrote this,
and this.

SEED

In the white bowl
the metal seed slid back

and forth through the blood,
making a red asterisk.

In the field where I killed
the deer, I planted

the mushroomed bullet.
Someday, someone might

find it and think:
metal statuette

honoring a nuclear explosion.
At a certain moment

the dream becomes
uncontrollable and

the wind forces
me to walk away.

Only to return
to this field in which

two bone-white trees
have grown. Each one

an echo of the other.

CHEKHOV'S GUN

Nothing ever absolutely has to happen. The gun
doesn't have to be fired. When our hero sits

on the edge of his bed contemplating the pistol
on his nightstand, you have to believe he might

not use it. Then the theatre is sunk in blackness.
The audience is a log waiting to be split open. The faint

scuff of feet. Objects are picked up, shuffled away.
Other things are put down. Based on the hushed sounds

you guess: a bed, some walls, a dresser. You feel
everything shift. You sense yourself being picked up,

set down. A cone of light cracks overhead. The audience's
eyes flicker toward you like droplets of water.

II

ELEGY IN X PARTS

Why do you rend me?
—Canto XIII, "Inferno"

X

Listen, the branch said,
and I heard inside

the silence of the tree.
The forest was crowned

in gnashing birds
but wore them well. I mean,

what's a little more pain
when pain's eternal? A tree

grieves by losing leaves,
but their abandoned bodies

reclaimed, will hang again
from their branches

like empty and elegant suits.

X

The mystery
begins like this:

We are more likely
to kill ourselves

than be killed
by someone else.

I am the pistol
saying, *I will only*

say this once.
Do not open

the tiny door
in the back

of your head.
All alone when

all alone, we
are asleep

inside our
murderer. There's

a metal word
in the chamber

of my mouth
and my eyes

are bored out.
I'm a noose

using the body
against itself.

I see
what's too awful

to be true—
that house

with its one lit window,
my brother's

punctured skull—
yet is.

X

I found a small ring
of your black hair

in the shower.
It could have been

worn like a laurel
by a mole

or hung like a wreath
on death's tiny door.

X

Your hands were delivered with the mail like postcards. There was
nothing written on them, but I knew they had come from somewhere

far away, because all the fingernails were painted like stamps. I looked
at the backs of your hands as if they were landscapes and tried to enjoy

the sunset of your skin and riverbed veins, but could only wonder why
we don't have a word for the backs of our hands. I think I put them in

a drawer somewhere. Then they appeared in the glove basket, so I put
them on. I punched one hand into the other, staring into the foyer mirror.

I was in a movie about to beat someone up *real bad,* but I didn't actually
have to, it was just a movie. My face looked absurd in the mirror, and I

said, *Inside all our hands are smaller, more evil ones.* Even though you
aren't supposed to say anything true in a movie.

X

A glass jar
rolls down

concrete stairs
ringing

a dangerous
music whose

next note
could pull

the instrument
apart.

X

The black suit hanging
on my door asks me

to put it on. I do, but then
can't find my shadow.

When I step outside
I wear the night

like an enormous costume.

X

Your brother is dead,
but you don't know yet.

Your father enters
the locker room—

his face carved
from pale wood.

You can imagine
the tools used to shape

his expression.
Except his eyes.

Those are unfashioned.
They say what

his wooden mouth can't.

X

There was a thud at the window like a bird hit it,
but your hands lay shuddering in the grass instead.

I kept them in a shoebox for a long time. I forgot
where they were, thought I threw them away.

Then I found them in a pile of leaves I'd raked up.
I put them on and finished raking. From there, I lost track.

It seemed like they were always inside my coat pockets,
waiting for me, and I would slip them on, or I was already

wearing them and didn't notice. Once, as a joke, I think
they jerked the wheel toward oncoming traffic.

But they're just hands. They're innocent.
I put them away again. Years fell away. Maybe a decade.

One night, I found them on my bookshelf,
the thumbs bound with thread. I opened them

and wrote a poem across their palms. I called the poem
"Handscapes," my word for the backs of our hands.

I couldn't think of a better title, so I burned the book
of your hands in the woodstove. In the morning

my coat pockets were full of ash.

X

My foreshadow stretches
out in front of me.

We stand on the soles
of each other's feet.

I am a field
and there's a man

standing in the middle
of me saying,

*God is the sky pinning
me to my body.*

I am a man
and there is a field

under me saying,
A dead man makes

*love to the earth
by just lying there.*

X

Kafka said, *A book*
must be an axe

for the frozen sea
inside us, which sounds

great, but what good
is an axe against

a frozen sea?
Perhaps this is why

he said, while dying,
Destroy everything.

There is little comfort
in knowing there

are worse undertakings
than killing yourself.

Is it dangerous
to say these things?

I don't think so.
Or I do. Either way,

don't believe me.
There is no refuge

from yourself.

X

Like a crime,
a privacy invades

itself, commits
Thee End.

And then eternity
inside the silence

of a tree.

If I could relight

your ashes I would.
If you torch a forest

it grows right back.

X

My imagination erodes
my mind. Sometimes

I wander the shore
of my memory searching

for what I've set afloat
or buried, finding

only fragments of you
I've had to disremember.

A secret code I've been
meaning to forget.

Periphery of stars
darkened by focus,

a near miss is still a miss.
My memory of you

is all untrue. The rumor:
you had to shoot yourself

twice because the first bullet
ricocheted off your jaw

and snapped your collarbone
like a bough. Even if this

didn't happen, it did.

X

All night, snow fell
like ash through a glass of water.

Everyone's lawns sleep
under a large empty page.

On the way to the funeral home
I could feel your note

folded into my shirt pocket,
cupping my chest like a passport

from a country wiped
off the world. When we stop

to get gas I look at my hands.
I'm wearing your gloves.

Dad, alone in the cold
outside, waits for the tank

to fill. Across the street,
kids build a man out of snow.

III

OUTGOING

Our answering machine still played your message,
and on the day you died Dad asked me to replace it.

I was chosen to save us the shame of dead you
answering calls. *Hello, I have just shot myself.*

To leave a message for me, call hell. The clear cassette
lay inside the white machine like a tiny patient

being monitored or a miniature glass briefcase
protecting the scroll of lost voices. Everything barely

mattered and then no longer did. I pressed record
and laid my voice over yours, muting it forever

and even now. *I'm sorry we are not here,* I began.

LAND O' LAKES

A tinfoil lake rattles the sun
as a canoe crosses it

approaching my shore.
The Native American girl

walks toward me, kneels,
offers a golden box of butter,

and then she's on the box
I am holding.

Apparently, I've accepted.
Come, she says, *we will*

burn beauty into something
even more mesmeric.

It is evening inside
the refrigerator.

I lie down shivering
near the lake.

The giant red ring
hovers behind her,

generating warmth.
You must fall asleep

in your dream to wake up
in your life, she says.

I can hear the vegetables
dying in the crisper

and through the door,
the television weeping

openly, unashamed.

A POEM IN WHICH LEAVES AGAIN
FIGURE PROMINENTLY

I fall asleep, waking to find
a poem in which leaves

figure prominently. If you
tear all of the skin away

leaving only the veins,
they are miniature trees,

the poem says.
I nod off as it describes

snow falling, warm as living skin.
The poem is right though,

warm snow would be nice
to lie down and sleep in.

This leaf is *orange,*
my dream last night—*poorly lit.*

Yet the snow falling though it
was whiter than real snow,

which isn't really white at all
but the rejection of light before

it melts into puddles the color
of whatever hovers above.

BURIAL

I buried a light bulb
in the garden and a flower

of smoldering filaments
bloomed downward,

toward you. Grief comes
like patient lava

I always easily outrun
while our past becomes blank

as an empty parking lot.
You have been dead half

of my life, and yet you sit
at the kitchen table

in my apartment
with a prescription bottle

full of bullets, reading
the directions aloud:

Do not take on an empty stomach.
Take one capsule every 24 hours.

Side effects may include . . .
You look up at me

and rub your eyes,
but I'm not there.

APERTURE

Opposite of closure,
a suicide's grave

never grows over.
My imagination carves

each memory of you
smaller and smaller

into dust. The fall after
you murdered you,

I burned your letter
in a mound of leaves

on our lawn.
Blackened grass,

stairwell of ash,
a greener door

grows there now
but not in me.

THE MOON

floats like a document
without a single word.
When it slips under

the horizon's desk
we are left
with the definition

of *unilluminated*.
Sight gives way
to the sound

of two clouds
colliding, breaking
each other apart.

What might seem
far off in the distance
could be just beyond

the border of our skin
or just within it.
We can feel

a terrible war
flower open.
Each cloud

as determined,
past the bloodshed
of dawn, to wave

their national flag:
its solid, inspiring
blue.

NOTLOVE POEM FOR THE FENCE
AT THE END OF THE FIELD

> We love a rose because it will soon be gone.
> —Rod Serling

The last thing the world needs
is another love poem.

Overhead, the secret cloud
society moves in enormous

silence, foretelling us our past lives.
At the end of the field

the air has a charged taste
of rust about to take root,

wired barbs set to snag
against a future

that never arrives.
Suddenly and suddenly.

Wind cuts through the fence,
folds the grass over

revealing a billboard
on the horizon advertising,

Death Bed For Sale: free.

O

The city says 58 things
at the same time.

Like a diamond's facets—
each surface reflecting

while trapping a sliver of flame
inside its cut heart.

.   .   .   .

Far away, a loon's call—
the whistle of a knife

through water—bounces
off the house-sized white stone.

A remnant of what the glacier
ate before it died.

.   .   .   .

The boulevard's hallway of trees
pauses, allowing the train below

to breathe. The promenade
rises like an Indian burial mound

with a grated mouth
that sucks at the spoiled air.

.   .   .   .

When cleaning a grouse,
puncture the crop

to release the scent
of fresh clover.

.   .   .   .

The city, these towers,
a valley of windows, empty

shelves for hard light
where inside our body's body,

the architecture
of the diamond burns.

.   .   .   .

Autumn field, leafless
trees. Why do you look

like the roots of buildings
swallowed by the sky?

.   .   .   .

Love me,
said love.

Oh my god,
said god.

.   .   .   .

At the base
of each bare tree

someone has spilled
a bucket of shadow.

. . . .

The bus brakes squeal
like a mouse pinned

under a microphone.
The sky fills in

behind what has fallen.
O, says the moon.

PHONE

At the foot of your grave
I planted our black phone

wrapped up in its coiled cord.
I'd hoped its ring would

shudder upward and each blade
of grass become a chime, pealing.

But together we decide
which way the dream goes

like spilled water on a table
we carry across the room.

I wait for the lawn to ring
while the cord sprouts

and a receiver blooms
like a black cucumber.

No one is calling so
I put it to my ear

expecting the steady
dial tone of your voice

but hear only the dark
breathing of the dirt.

AN UNCERTAIN PRAYER

after Anna Kamienska

God let me forget the definition
of *kinematics*. Allow me

the power to change
nearly nothing. Make the world

completely ignorant
of the many sufferings

of tiny spiders
and let large waves

continually wreck
like sheets of porcelain.

Make your voice unheard
and lift your love off me

like a burning blanket.
Allow us the unclenching

of hands. God let me
no longer take up space

and let the space I free up
remain vacant.

YOUR BODY IS A TEMPLE IS A BODY AGAIN

Stained glass
depicts the holiness

of gun flash.
The tapestries hung

in the cathedral
honor the doom idol's

peeled-open, copper
face. To turn around

during "The Tapping
of the Divine Shoulder"

is a transgression.
In "The Sacred Image

at City Beach" you kneel
while your hands

are buried to the wrists.
Praise the hallowed

hollow-point, the negation
creation. "Thus Enters

the Holy Bullet."
Your worshippers' arms

float upward as though
tied to invisible birds.

Only they have no hands,
they've sunk them

into the sky.
I laid the cornerstone

over your deathface,
then we burned

your sanctuary
to the bone and poured

it down the ground's
black throat. Your life

was just a doorway,
and hovering above you

a red voice urging
EXIT.

O CREMULATOR

The crematorium leaves
bone chunks on its tongue

among the ash we've become.
We cannot bear the weight

of our own imaginations
and so we must be fractured

further. O cremulator,
o cocktail of potable sand,

your steel bearings grind us
all to the same granule.

Do the work of the dirt
but with passion.

At every moment
we are broken in half

and then half again, and then
one shadow melts into another,

one ashtray spills into the next.
We burn early into the morning.

The crematorium releases
its thread of smoke

into the bluing air.
We imagine ourselves

sewn into the sunrise
and the numb sky

whispering to the smoke,
climb, but nothing escapes,

everything eventually settles.
All that remains is our resin

on the walls, a thin film
that builds on the retort's bricks

until, according to routine,
they're dismantled and replaced.

AFTER SUICIDE

At the party celebrating me,
you always show up late

and dead. Ding-Dong.
Ding-Dong. No one

gets the door; we know
better. You let yourself in,

sidle up to people
who never knew you

and tell them jokes.
I have such terrible aim,

I had to shoot myself twice.
Three suicidal Norwegians

walk into a bar.
The first one complains

of a splitting headache
and orders a beer,

a gun, and two bullets.
I've heard it. We all have.

Unable to ignite even
a sizzle of laughter

you put a flashlight
into your mouth

and turn it on.
On the wall behind you,

a coin of light hovers
like the miniature sun

a magnifying glass makes.
Your head's a projector

showing the movie
of your death. We sip

our drinks with unease
as, luckily, the wall begins

to smoke and everyone runs
out onto the cool lawn

to watch the house burn,
relieved you're still inside.

REVERSE SUICIDE

The guy Dad sold your car to
comes back to get his money,

leaves the car. With filthy rags
we rub it down until it doesn't shine

and wipe your blood into
the seams of the seat.

Each snowflake stirs before
lifting into the sky as I

learn you won't be dead.
The unsuffering ends

when the mess of your head
pulls together around

a bullet in your mouth.
You spit it into Dad's gun

before arriving in the driveway
while the evening brightens

and we pour bag after bag
of leaves on the lawn,

waiting for them to leap
onto the bare branches.

A HORSE GRAZES IN MY SHADOW

after James Wright

Startled by my breath it bolts
to the other end of the field.

The horizon's brow rasps
against a green cloud,

which seems both
desperate and sincere.

Into a dead tree
a flame of bird

drives its burning beak.
And somewhere out here

I have come to terms
with my brother's suicide.

I wish the god of this place
would put me in its mouth

until I dissolve, until
the field doesn't end

and I am broken down
like a rifle,

swabbed clean.

ACKNOWLEDGMENTS

Grateful acknowledgment goes to the following journals and anthologies in which these poems, or earlier versions of them, originally appeared:

Dislocate: "Tom Black"; *Everyday Genius:* "And God Said,"; *Great Twin Cities Poetry Read,* Vol. 2: "An Uncertain Prayer"; *Gulf Coast:* "Land O' Lakes," and from "Elegy in X Parts": "X" ("The mystery begins like this . . ."), "X" ("Your hands were delivered with the mail . . ."), and "X" ("Kafka said, *A book* . . ."); *H_NGM_N:* "A Poem in which Leaves again Figure Prominently" and "Your Body Is A Temple Is A Body Again"; *LIT:* "I Am Not a Poem"; *MARGIE:* "After Suicide" ("At the party celebrating me . . ."), and from "Elegy in X Parts": "X" ("I found a small ring . . .") as "After Suicide" and "Burial" as "After Suicide"; *Mid-American Review:* "O Cremulator"; *New York Quarterly:* "Field with Whales" as "This Place"; *Oyez Review:* "After Suicide" ("A hole is nothing . . .") as "Dream After Suicide"; *Paper Darts:* "Aperture," "The Moon," "Seed," and "Vacation Cage"; *Passages North:* "Reverse Suicide"; *Poet Lore:* "Trajectory" as "Bullet"; *Poetry Daily:* from "Elegy in X Parts": "X" ("The mystery begins like this . . ."), "X" ("Your hands were delivered with the mail . . ."), and "X" ("Kafka said, *A book* . . ."); *Poetry Midwest:* "O"; *Poets.org:* "A Horse Grazes in My Shadow," "Chekhov's Gun," "In Whoever's Hotel Room this Is," and from "Elegy in X Parts": "X" ("Kafka said, *A book* . . .") and "X" ("My foreshadow stretches . . ."); *Redivider:* "Monet as a Verb," "The Orange Leaves," and "We're Not the Stars, We're What's Between Them"; *Water~Stone Review:* "747" as "Composed Upon a 747," "Outgoing," "Phone," and from "Elegy in X Parts": "X" ("*Listen,* the branch said . . ."), "X" ("A glass jar . . ."), "X" ("The black suit hanging . . ."), "X" ("There was a thud at the window . . ."), "X" ("My imagination erodes . . ."), and "X" ("All night, snow fell . . ."); *What Light: This Week's Poem:* "After Suicide" ("In the hallway of life . . .") as "Titled."

The poems "After Suicide" ("In the hallway of life . . ."), "After Suicide" ("A hole is nothing . . ."), "Field With Whales," "Notlove Poem for the Fence at the End of the Field," "O," "Reverse Suicide," and "Trajectory" all appeared in their current or previous versions under their current or previous titles in *Fingergun,* a chapbook from Kitchen Press (2006).

"Land O' Lakes" appeared on Minnesota Public Radio's *Writing Minnesota* hosted by Annie Baxter.

"Trajectory" appeared on PEN.org as part of the PEN Poetry Series.

"After Suicide" ("At the party celebrating me . . ."), "Elegy in X Parts": "X" ("I found a small ring . . .") as "After Suicide," "Land O' Lakes," "Outgoing," and "Reverse Suicide" were all recorded for the Knox Writer's House Recording Project (*www.knoxwritershouse.com*).

Note: The poem "Tom Black" amalgamates several events including three tragic suicides that occurred in International Falls, MN. I offer my condolences to the families of Tom Black and Bobby Hamalainen.

Special thanks to Jane Hirshfield and the Academy of American Poets for making this book a reality.

Thank you also to LSU Press, particularly Neal Novak and John Easterly.

This book would not be possible without the love and support of so many people. I'm sorry if I have forgotten anyone.

Thank you to my parents, Allen and Gail; my wife, Jana; and daughter, Lydia; Chris Tonelli; Dan Boehl; Justin Marks; Sam Starkweather; Sarah Bartlett; Emily Frey; Elisa Gabbert; Kathy Rooney; Abby Beckel; Caryn Lazzuri; Chad Reynolds; Kate Covintree; Alexis Orgera; Ben Mirov; Chris Martin; Nate Pritts; Alyce Mannausau; Linda Faith; Darrell Schmidt; Roy Miskulin; Dick Ostroot; David Skwarok; Jim Moore; Arthur Sze; Robert Hedin; Pete Hautman; Jerod Santek; Lisa Higgs; Michelle Pollock; Nena Johansen; Michael Morse; Charlie Conley; Matt Ryan; Matt Mauch; Phil Bryant; Joyce Sutphen; John Rezmerski; Will Freiert; Dan Tobin; Gail Mazur; John Skoyles; Bill Knott; Malachi Black; Patricia Kirkpatrick; Art Przybilla; Baker Lawley; Alex Dimitrov; Kitchen Press; and all the members of the West Fork Literary Society.

Thank you for accommodation, time, or financial support from The McKnight Foundation, The Minnesota State Arts Board, Ernest Oberholtzer's Mallard Island, The Bush Foundation, The Corporation of Yaddo, The Loft Literary Center, The Jerome Foundation, Intermedia Arts, and The Anderson Center in Red Wing, MN.

Matt Rasmussen is a fiscal year 2011 recipient of an Artist Initiative grant from the Minnesota State Arts Board. This activity was made possible in part by a grant from the Minnesota State Arts Board, through an appropriation by the Minnesota State Legislature and by a grant from the National Endowment for the Arts.